Peace

is Possible

Joseph Raffa

Peace is Possible

Author: Joseph Raffa

Editor: Teena Raffa-Mulligan

ISBN 978-0-9944990-2-8

eISBN 978-0-9944990-9-7

Author's note: The term 'mankind' as used throughout this discourse is a reference to the human race collectively.

Published by Sea Song Publications

sea-song@bigpond.com

www.seasongpublications.com

1.

VIOLENCE in its various forms is a feature of the human expression that deeply disturbs sensitive people. There is something repellently ugly about unprovoked violence, the kind that strikes without warning, is brutally conducted and leaves its victims bruised, broken, raped and sometimes dead. The persistence of the assailants, regardless of pleas for mercy and mindless of the injuries sustained by those on the receiving end of the attacks, indicates a callous disregard towards suffering that is bewildering to those who cannot act in this way.

Human nature at the best of times is such a warm, enriching experience that flows with consideration, togetherness and good humour. Such a stark contrast to the behaviour that follows when violence is on the rampage. What makes such destructive releases possible? Regardless of the circumstances that lead to its expression, the propensity for violence is a latent possibility, to some degree, in every human mind, except in those who have been spiritually inoculated against its release. Children too are not immune to its impact and have been known to do surprising things. Perhaps adults have set too ready an example.

When the capacity for violence is in its quiescent state it gives no visible sign of its awesome potential. At such times, humans go about their business, laughing, working and showing an agreeable face to the crowd. Yet in humans prone to violence, there is a time bomb of sorts, primed with a fuse, long or short. It only takes the prodding of circumstances or experience, contact with disturbing challenges, or the devilish ingenuity of desire and thinking to light the fuse and the spark of impulse travels without restraint to the inflammable mixture of expendable violence. The result is a physical, verbal, emotional or mental explosion. Disruption or damage usually follows in varying degrees of intensity. When the disruption remains on the verbal level, people manage to cope, even though this may be for some, if sustained, extremely unpleasant, emotionally unbalancing and mentally draining.

There is a violence that hides unnoticed in the crowd. It surveys the human scene like a spider spinning a web to trap the unwary. Its face is the ordinary face that humans wear. It may reflect a smile, talk in friendly fashion and give no indication of what lies beneath. Cold and calculating this kind of violence, unfeeling and merciless without the slightest touch of pity when it strikes. Out of its brutal expression come the most hideous murders, sometimes preceded by prolonged torture and before the perpetrators are caught, may lead to a series of multiple killings selected at random.

These are the murders that deeply shock society. People shake their heads in disbelief and psychiatrists reach out for some kind of reasonable evaluation to explain this kind of behaviour in rational terms. But there isn't any kind of explanation that will calm the outrage people feel in the wake of such crimes, particularly for those who are close to the victims. The feeling of helplessness, the sadness of the loss, the unbelievable nature of the violence, the tragic impact of a combination of consequences are deeply felt by those who knew the victims well. And when the events settle and justice has had its way, those who were closely related return to face shattered lives left empty and devastated by a loss they do not understand.

Society contains the evildoers as best it can, either through long years of confinement or through execution, depending on the laws in vogue at the time. Still, we are left with the unpalatable fact that society has no protection against such outrages. In spite of police protection, modern psychiatric knowledge and laws to deal with the situations that arise, monsters in human form emerge to strike at unsuspecting victims, regardless of any consequences.

Must society always wait until these crimes happen, always be on the receiving end before it can act with protective measures that defuse this ugly potential before it manifests physically? Is there any kind of education that offers humans at least the possibility of understanding and dealing with its early stages in the human expression before it explodes on the social scene? These are questions that trouble those who are concerned with human behaviour, who long to see an improvement in human relationships.

But the most difficult thing to understand is why? Why are people so prone to resort to violence, to brutal, barbaric violence? In its most violent aspects there can be no doubt in sensitive minds as to the morally degrading nature of what is happening. Surely even those who at times perpetrate the most cowardly and savage attacks on fellow humans, without cause, must at some time realise the wrongness of what they do. They may camouflage the results with prejudice fashioned to support their brutal activity, yet deep down there must be a spark of acknowledgement that what they do is beyond acceptable human behaviour. Particularly when they look at the battered victims, at the results of their unrestrained attacks.

How they live with the guilt, with the vivid images, and continue to plot more of the same shows a debasement beyond human credibility. Are some born with this capacity or does it develop through some derangement of the mind under pressure of disturbing and disagreeable experiences? Many are capable of verbal violence, even a blow or two, but the majority would shrink from murder, rape or extreme forms of violence. Except during wartime when killing and the destruction of property are condoned, even legalised to protect the national boundaries and the interests of the nation. The physical training and mental indoctrination undergone by men and women encourages people to accept and express violence and destruction for the duration of war.

So much so that there appears to be little hesitation in carrying out the necessities of duty even if this means the annihilation of civilians via mass shelling of cities or saturation raids by aircraft. Somehow, killing from a distance depersonalises the whole ugly business and does not involve human sensibilities to the same extent as hand to hand encounters whereby combatants are in close proximity and must face each other's final moments with no weakening of intention.

What those involved think and feel about the taking of human life when the passions raised by war have subsided is a matter of some interest to those who follow the human expression through the changing aspects of its behaviour. The brutal nature of war is explained by necessity, by the national and personal need to survive intact. Reluctant or otherwise, members of the armed forces accept the logic of a kill or be killed attitude. This hardens the heart and protects the mind from doubts about the causes it is committed to.

Once released, the destructive power of technology in the hands of organised intent is awesome to behold. What the long-term effects of prolonged expressions of violence are on the human psyche even long after hostilities are over is a matter that requires deep introspection, not only by combatants but also by those who help those suffering the after effects. Many put aside the effect of years of licence to slaughter and return to civilian life without disturbing psychological reactions. Others wander in a no man's land of unsettled behaviour, disturbed by what they have seen and done.

Occasionally, there are suicides by those who cannot condone the part they played in past destructive activity. Also outbreaks of a senseless slaughter of innocents by others unbalanced by wartime experiences who still carry the scars of combat deep inside. Yet when it has been analysed and studied from all angles, after conclusions have been formulated, we are still puzzled by the arousal and continuance of violence. Why its persistence, the acceptance of it as a necessary expression by those who undertake to carry out its directives whatever these may be? Particularly when a gentle, caring life has so much to offer in comparison.

2.

SELF DEFENCE is a compelling argument in its favour. What then of those who initiate it, who under no immediate threat to themselves become like brigands on the prowl, killing where the mind directs? Violence must serve an imperative need in the lives of those who act in this way. A twisted need it must be, yet still a powerful and compelling one, else why would they give way to it?

How would we eradicate such a powerful bent in the human expression? Not with violence which only feeds the fires of this kind of misdirected energy, but with the unfolding of a different order of understanding if this is at all possible. In dealing with the lesser forms of violence that happen in society, those in control do what they can by enacting laws that define its expression, the degree of severity and the penalties to be paid by those who transgress. But this is a measure of containment, of removing the violent from the social scene for a time. It is not an inducement towards total eradication. Society's means are limited until definite acts of violence are committed. Unless threats by one person against another are such as to raise the conviction in the mind of a judge that there is a danger to innocent people, society does not act until after the outbreak. By then, it is too late for the victim.

Societies have systems of education and legislative frameworks that seek to provide the means whereby thoughtful people are given some kind of foundation to accept lawful living and the putting aside of unduly selfish and violent considerations. By the imposition of social disciplines and the adoption of moral frameworks, individuals and thereby the community mutually benefit. The antagonistic qualities of human nature are recognised. The control of aggressive behaviour is a necessary prerequisite for peaceful living otherwise chaos results.

The intention to educate in this direction and create a moral basis for inter-relationships is sincere and is the focus of a great deal of thought. Not only by the state but also by parents who are in the position to influence by example and by discussion as children develop. Some manage better than others in the learning experience that follows. Behavioural results vary even though school education is uniformly offered. Parents too have been exposed to a widespread, socially acceptable level of behaviour which has been adopted and in turn passed on to their children. Continuity of experience in this manner helps to encourage uniformity and the acceptance of the moral standards prevailing in the community.

This combined approach by state and parents is the developing framework through which people endeavour to provide a happy and meaningful medium for relating and working with each other. It is complex, with many ramifications. Basically what it means is that people desire an orderly life undisturbed by anything ugly so they can, within the protection afforded by the state, pursue the ideas, intentions and lifestyles considered important.

This is successful to a degree. Yet in spite of constant learning, reflection and discussion it fails to bring the social conditions longed for by the more sensitive. Some societies are extremely unstable and violence is a continuing theme even though those who are involved recognise the obvious benefits to be gained by peaceful living. Others are stable as regards internal violence on a large scale yet are unsettled by riots, strikes and recurring individual expressions that surface from time to time to disrupt any prospect of undisturbed harmony.

Although violence can be contained to a degree and those who transgress are punished when apprehended, it cannot be confidently stated that humans are in control to the extent that violence is no longer a disturbing fact of day to day existence. Somewhere, somehow, it suddenly strikes. And unfortunately it has the disconcerting characteristics of a bush fire on the international scene. A spark is ignited in one place, a conflagration begins and burns through inflammable human material, often crossing frontiers with impunity until it has run its destructive course.

Is humanity doomed to go on projecting a variable expression of violence as an inevitable aspect of its nature? Were we born to behave like this? Are we expressing something deeply implanted by nature, something impossible to eradicate, that must be suffered and endured for as long as humans interact in social living? We observe the savage behaviour of animals in defence of their kind, the protection of their territory and in killing for food. Rarely though do we see the organised slaughter to match what humans do when they war against their own kind. Humans, with calculated brutality and psychologically applied fiendish tortures are way out on their own with the prolonged suffering they inflict. Some gain a perverse satisfaction in what they do and bring to bear a devilish ingenuity to plan and then spur their actions.

Neither fear, moral sense, nor spark of arresting conscience act as a deterrent. In fact, laws in some countries are often framed to permit inquisitions to force confessions from those suspected of being a threat or enemies of the established authorities. With reflection, one is compelled to ask, "Did nature go astray in some way to create monsters in human forms?"

Or is it that we are as yet in a low stage of human development and not far enough removed from a former primitive and savage ancestry? If we are religiously inclined we may also ask, "Did God foul up somewhere along the line to allow such human behaviour?" Yet this doesn't fit the image of God as all loving and all wise.

Has it some hidden purpose, this persistent capacity for violence, this evil expression that will not fade in spite of human intention? Does it show that going it alone without contact with a higher power, people are helpless to control and transform human nature and incapable of banishing violence to the dusty attic of past and finished human history?

We are creatures of reason. We desire to understand. We are not easily satisfied with explanations unless they are effective in improving human behaviour. Is it true then, that without reconnecting with a higher nature, humans go haywire, because there isn't any intelligent directive to infuse and inspire their day to day living? Is that why destructive tendencies take root, fester and grow to eventually erupt into erratic and undesirable social activity? That we behave this way because we lack the deeper insights that arise in the human expression when contact with the spiritual source is ongoing from day to day?

If this is true, what can we do to realise the truth of this, not through verbal statements that are easily read and memorised but through discovery, so we are there, one with it and reveling in what it brings? People cannot be forced to return against their will. If inclined they will continue to behave as though kin with devilish intentions rather than a divine one and behave accordingly. How then do we break the hold of this power to monopolise humans for destructive ends? Is there a need of a new education, beginning with the young before undesirable and insidious attitudes become too deeply established to be easily eradicated? Can the young be educated differently unless parents and teachers have also accepted and absorbed it and thereby live differently and demonstrate by example the value of what they have?

I write here not of technical education in all its variety, but of moral values based on spiritual discovery, with the realisation of Oneness as the basis for living. This is a vibrant, dynamic learning about the mind, the self in social relationships. As it takes hold, it covers every aspect of social and individual conditioning. It is an inner exploration of what takes place within, covering motivation, thinking, feeling, desire. Nothing is missed as the ways of the self are relentlessly investigated by an eager intention to discover truth and nothing but the truth about what is going on in the human expression. To lodge in the Silent Heart of what we are is the high ideal pursued, to grow closer and closer and to stay there, regardless of what transpires on the surface.

This is not an education primarily concerned with achievement, with being a top dog in whatever we do. Its aim is to deepen understanding of the human expression, to shift the attention from its anchorage in the known where it is confined to the surface, and set it adrift in the deeper levels of the human content. It covers the totality of how we function day by day and shifts the emphasis from narrow self-interest, from aggressive and selfish considerations to a reflection of gentler qualities, harmony and love for mankind.

State education ignores the spiritual potential. It focuses on developing people into moving smoothly into the social machines that exist today. Not enough encouragement is given to the investigation of erratic behaviour, how it gains its sustenance from the limited standpoint of a self that is sundered from its universal source. Social equilibrium and individual balance are being assailed by destructive tendencies, bitter divisions and antagonistic and critical debates. Violence creeps in, infiltrating one to one relationships and expanding through organisation to influence state, national and international affairs. Verbal violence is tolerated as part of life, but the accusations, the savage criticisms may suddenly change from a war of words into overt aggression and peaceful intentions rapidly flee before this kind of onslaught.

3.

ITHIN the nature of those who are swayed towards violence lies the trigger of attitudes and influences that primes the reactions we understand as violent. The release may take its time but as sure as night follows day, some form of antagonistic response will emanate from those who neglect to understand the behaviour and interaction that develops when people come together in some kind of relationship. Society has its moral standards and ideas of right and wrong. There are complex laws to cover what can and can't be done and penalties for infringements. Parents try by example and discussion to give their children a basis for living that will be a reliable guide as they grow and venture out into the social mainstream.

Schools enhance this with an education that gives some kind of stability and a foundation on which to mould present action and to shape a future that will satisfy material needs, a variety of interests and perhaps higher aspirations for something more out of life than financial security and material rewards. Students are given goals to aim for that include refined behaviour, playing the game according to recognised rules of fair play and the reaching out for success and positions of prominence. They are also encouraged to be compassionate, to consider others less fortunate and to live and work in a spirit of service to the community rather than to grasp single-mindedly for the self's sake.

These are honourable intentions by parents and the education system, yet somehow they fail to create the reliable grounding that consistently guides the younger generation into happy and vibrant adulthood, free of disturbing complications. This may be because the young do not properly understand and absorb the learning offered, or the teaching is not administered from the highest level of self-discovery: spontaneously as the need arises, in ongoing discussions in which teachers and students come together in a spirit of mutual learning. Then again, the young may insist on going their own way and not show any interest in pursuing the theme of self-discovery to its natural culmination, regardless of encouragement. They may prefer instead to opt for a social life with its attendant advantages of security, material benefits and a host of variable pursuits to make life interesting.

Whatever the reason for failing to address the need for inner development, many fall by the wayside and ignore the calling to a higher purpose.

Consequently there is little impetus given to gaining the spiritual foundations and insights into the human character that effectively defuse the potential for violent and destructive activity. While society does its best to contain violence and erratic behaviour with the means at its disposal, it takes, in the main, a surface view of the situation and does not essentially consider the inner nature of the human expression in these disturbing directions.

It is, after all, within the mind that reactions are initiated and although this is acknowledged to a degree, it is through reasonable discussion and analysis from a surface standpoint that people of skill and learning hope to stem the flow of violence into the outer surrounds. Self-understanding is a difficult undertaking at the best of times. Even when we are voluntarily and totally committed to this undertaking, the learning process is littered with pitfalls, illusions and mental barriers that retard progress. In the case of those who show no interest and prefer to pursue their inclinations in living regardless of where this leads them, the new learning doesn't even get the necessary support to take off.

Without any depth in self-understanding, not only of the easily identified surface aspects but also with the inward nature, what can teachers or students hope to accomplish in translating a learning of consequence into harmonious social action? Self-understanding implies a journey of exploration — a getting to know ourselves so that we are not strangers to what goes on in the private precinct of our individual expression. It is not a journey made under compulsion or pressure, with exams and marks given, but an undertaking of interest, of a deep desire to learn about the self and its processes. Nor is the learning a complex psychological one with difficult terminology but a direct and simple unfolding — of being naturally aware of our reactions as they arise in response to the moving panorama of life that is ever present around us.

It also means disentanglement from the conditioning power of ideas and words and a shift from the surface level of understanding with its over-riding capacity to impose its own particular vision on everything it comes into contact with. The surrounding social influences that have infiltrated the mind since its first moments of conscious awareness need to be put aside as well. Otherwise the mind will continue to linger in false perception and the true will pass it by. This is a day to day commitment with the express intention of investigating the total human content, not only those aspects that are pleasing but also those that are disturbing. This is not a game of playing favourites, of ignoring the unpleasant aspects of our behaviour.

As explorers travelling the territory of the mind and its inter-related activities, we do not pick and choose where to cast the spotlight of a searching attention. Rather, we go where the spirit of learning takes us regardless of consequences. Truth is the shining star that attracts, glowing brightly from afar, drawing us away from ignorance and misunderstanding. The highest levels of insight and self-discovery are the earnest considerations of the spiritual seeker.

Without insight and a deep grounding in self-discovery, the self falls prey to misunderstanding and misconception. Dark moods and darker deeds erupt in the unstable and the imagination becomes the instrument of disruptive, selfish and aggressive tendencies. Not recognising its spiritual connection, Self wanders in a no-man's land of fear, concerns and desires. Ideas are given pre-eminence and dominate mankind's movement. The constraints of mind-devised disciplines, rather than a spontaneous appraisal of a spiritual understanding guide human actions or intentions. With the mind wide open since birth, surrounding social influences pour in and make of the human material a particular mould that fits in with social intention.

Within this overlay, the self acts and initiates its courses of action. Mostly, it is content to operate within the boundaries inculcated since birth. Although it may press against these boundaries from time to time, even transgress in minor ways of little consequence, at times the social movement is brutally disrupted by antagonisms, perverse behaviour and violence of the most shocking kind. The self may not be clearly aware of its capacity in these directions nor even consider it is capable of disarranged behaviour. Yet years of social restraints and steady behaviour have been forcefully thrust aside when wars erupt and the all clear is given for violence and destruction to proceed with little restriction until the issue has been eventually settled.

People will argue that war is a matter of individual and national survival, that little choice is allowed as to whether they should be involved. It is still a brutally destructive way to settle differences and significantly points to a lack of understanding, of harmony and a peaceful disposition between humans. It is also a sign that education is failing to produce spiritually integrated and happy people, in tune with the universal nature and deeply considerate of others and their different social standing. It indicates too, that violence, even as a last resort, is considered an effective and acceptable means to bring about desirable conclusions in human affairs. It is terminal for many and does bring about temporary results that at first sight offer the means to rebuild on new and peaceful foundations. Inevitably, because the inner strains in human relationships have not been dealt with from a basis of consideration and understanding, they surface anew after a period of incubation to breed more of the destruction and violence that is accepted as an enduring theme of human behaviour.

4.

SO INGRAINED is this concept in the human psyche that in the kind of world we live in today, the means of combating violence is to resort to highly trained and organised personnel. Always held in a state of readiness, they can be swiftly deployed to retaliate in like kind should hostilities eventuate. As a consequence, violence rumbles and reverberates around our troubled earth. Individually, it stalks and strikes, in an organised way it runs riot and perhaps only the threat of atomic retaliation prevents wider outbreaks. Meanwhile, lesser wars wax and wane in intensity, sometimes stubbornly persisting for years with an intractability that defies diplomatic intentions to resolve the deep-rooted differences that gave birth to these monstrous examples of human behaviour.

To keep the cauldron of violence simmering, isolated cases erupt as a reminder that nowhere is sacrosanct, no life inviolate, as innocents young and old are senselessly slaughtered to appease the lust for violent expression. Out of the human ranks they come, those who are controlled by the urge to kill and destroy on demand — or command. And kill they do, relentlessly, unfeelingly, even people they do not know, who have not done them harm, till their own lives are taken or the blood lust exhausts itself.

Society is left wondering, shocked and disturbed, with questions following about the best means of containment. With individual cases there are suggestions to bring back the lash, the death sentence, gaol perpetrators for life or tighten gun laws. Sadly, whatever means are employed from the outer they do not touch the inner, do not transform human nature, and those intent on violence still find the means and the way to express this side of their nature.

Humankind must decide whether to keep working away at the surface aspects of violence with changing laws or whether to confront it in the depths of the human expression where it is birthed and festers until it forges an outlet. This means we must be shock troopers, in the front line of an inner battle, each taking responsibility for whatever we project in the field of human relationships. For as surely as each person withdraws support from violent endeavour and self- centred considerations that are disruptive and antagonistic, so these expressions will lose power little by little till they fade and die away.

A peaceful world in every way can only follow if we are truly peaceful people. Not only peaceful as the mind understands this but a deeper enduring peace where every propensity for violence has been eradicated by a developing spiritual understanding. In this, violence is no longer a part of the human expression, not just quietly marking time until the next outbreak. This kind of understanding is given birth in those strange moments of timeless communion with the Eternal when the self as we know it, in all its ramifications, its sense of separation, vanishes for a moment and the universal nature reigns undisturbed. In this meeting, that which has identified with the known aspects of the self and has taken itself to be body — name — disentangles itself from its timeful connection and returns to its universal source.

Strange and inexplicable as these moments are, they act like a catalyst, pouring fresh waves of insight into the human expression. The shadowy aspects of self-behaviour are thrown into sharp relief. Hidden elements and underlying motivations, formerly unsuspected, are exposed. These influences, garnered from society and individual disposition have settled into the unconscious extent of human nature. This is a subtle grafting process. Habitual acceptance and ready identification, consciously and unconsciously permitted, allow unhindered establishment. In the inner extent, there is no sense of being separate from acquired influences, and the complex background of attitudes that have interwoven with the self form the matrix from which the movement into time, social surrounds and relationships is launched.

It is this background, forged into purposeful actions by the self in response to surrounding stimuli that determines the nature of behaviour and the reactions that follow. Whether people are peaceful and gentle is mainly influenced by the measure of understanding developed about the background content and its influence. Although constantly expanding, modifying and changing direction, the purpose of serving the self with what it desires or chooses is constantly maintained. This is the only way it functions and this may be for worthwhile or higher purposes when spiritually awake or for destructive, debasing or selfish ends when spiritually asleep.

The issue of violence in society has been tackled in various ways. Over the years of social interaction, moral standards of behaviour have been developed. People are expected to adhere to these.

The standards apply to individual relationships, extend to property and financial transactions, to organisations and political behaviour and range into international affairs. The governing laws are complex and extensive. In the wake of this expanding complexity there are established courts, a system of justice and experienced personnel to interpret and preside over the transgressions or differences that arise and need resolution.

Citizens are expected to understand the laws and their application in human affairs. While the verbal explicitness of the arrangements is understood, what is not always understood from a deeper level is human nature, the stubbornness of it and its insistence to do the acts or things that are strictly forbidden. Not only by the laws of the land, but also by a moral sense that has its grounding in years of living experience; and perhaps too, by reference to a religious background which has a heritage of rules of behaviour framed to improve the quality of living together.

In the deeper extent of human nature we are left to grope our way. We are expected to get by on thou shall or thou shall not. Yet often people are drawn in directions that serve little worthwhile purpose. They may even know this, yet still yield to powerful attractions of temptation dressed up by the mind in such a seductive manner that the mind is drawn in spite of its misgivings and uncertainty. The demand to experience, to have and to desire are compelling factors in human nature. Self-protection too, is very powerful and this can be undertaken in particularly violent ways to preserve national boundaries, possessions, the self and its standing. And often, after violent expression, some are left nursing feelings of guilt if sensitively inclined, or with a sense of having behaved badly. Yet at the time when reactions are in full control, no rational or reasonable restraint operates to halt the headlong rush into confrontations or explosive situations.

Clearly then, before reactions by word or deed take over, there is a blockage between the assessments that lead to affrays and the possibility of calm reflection being in charge. There may be grounds for excuse when control is lost, provided the damage is minimal. Planned actions that lead to murder, rape and extreme cases of violence can never be excused. Here, it would seem that there is often time for second thoughts and for a reversal of the intended direction. Yet the commitment is so powerful that the controlling factor persists despite the time lag between the decision and the culmination of the intention.

Where the objective is intended brutality, there must be a measure of conditioning beforehand. And the acceptance that such will indeed be the involvement to be undertaken. If those predisposed this way are not mentally hardened and their sensibilities distorted prior to such acts, could they contemplate, let alone undertake actions of predetermined callous brutality? A perversion of human nature is abroad, a grave dislocation from the essential unifying nature that permeates all life with its remarkable essence of Being. Otherwise dark deeds could not be undertaken. It is not natural for humans to behave in these ways. Regardless of our long history in this direction, this behaviour is not a birthright, something we are compelled towards.

Estrangement from the universal source has led to self-dislocation and gross self-emphasis. It has closed the door to a wider awareness of the living process, narrowed the mind down to feeding its appetites for experience, sensation and stimulation. It has precluded finer considerations of another's feelings, of another's desire to live undisturbed by ugly and unwarranted intrusion. Without reconnection, people live in obscurity, in the shadows cast by the mind. Self-awareness cannot break free from its timeful connections, cannot expand from its base in the shadows and shift into the full glow of the Sunshine of Being.

All manner of afflictions take root. Living is blighted in so many ways. We struggle every which way to put things right, but the dark side insists on its outlet. Its capacity for disruption must be ended by an enlightened understanding if peaceful living is to settle into individual lives and by extension, cover this planet with its blessings and benediction. And this enlightenment comes only from spiritual discovery, not by the laws and arrangements of the mind.

5.

VIOLENCE on an individual scale, though damaging, is limited and confined in scope. On an international scale it rapidly spreads to encompass millions of people and vast expanses of territory, becoming global in its implications and effects. The human intellect, welded and powered by organisation, allied with science, has become a most effective instrument of violent expression. The destruction wrought by modern armies has magnified enormously in this century and the cemeteries of the battlefields are lined with the dead of many battles.

Nearly every country has its monuments to its war heroes. Their deeds are commemorated annually and shrines to honour the dead have been built. They are preserved with care and accorded solemn respect. The man with the rifle and bayonet, dressed in battle gear, is revered as the nation's saviour. Rarely are men of peace the idols to look up to, but men of war, of action, of violent action. It has sometimes been said by men of distinction that the greatest sacrifice of all is to sacrifice one's life for the nation, for one's countrymen. The sacrifices of human life in war are well known. We take notice of these and acknowledge the courage displayed.

There is another kind of sacrifice, a much more difficult one. This yields, through voluntary submission to a higher directive, every expectation and intention to sustain and expand the self; to persist in its individual isolation; to hold tenaciously to valued attachments, cherished ideas, traditions, national implants; and to the insistence to persist individually on a psychological level in an acknowledged and distinctive way. This is a special kind of dying, a death that precedes rebirth in a spiritual dimension of existence. It is a giving over by the mind of its established position of prominence in the human expression so that a spiritual directive takes over to rule the human entity. Not only is this for the benefit of the individual who yields but also for the benefit of others in that harm is not done to them, not even inadvertently.

Death on the battlefield is final. In this, there is no spiritual flowering nor the opportunity for renewal. Only a sad record of events, a tearful and solemn remembrance and a time for mourning. The death that leads to renewal has tremendous significance, an importance beyond the mind's measure. There is a vital learning initiated. It leads to a gentle and peaceful expression and dissolves the aggressive intent of the self with the understanding it releases. Harmony and cooperation in relationships begin to flourish in day to day living. Not by conscious intention of the mind does this eventuate but as a natural consequence of what follows when, not physical death takes place, but the strange coming to an end that happens when all forms of self-identification and self-activity are spontaneously put aside.

The vast fabric of the mind's attachment with experience, people, places, its mental and physical images, whatever illusions have taken hold, all vanish. Mind is in a vacuum of non-action, the relative effect of experience has lost its hold and we are nowhere and no-when without sense of being anything at all. Everything that was formerly so dominant — attitudes and desires, compelling demands and driving ambitions, disturbing moods, problems, difficulties, dark and ugly projections, the busy go go of timeful activity — are snuffed out as effectively as a candle flame is extinguished by a single puff.

Who would desire a death that is the end of the individual overlay? Who would initiate the kind of education that would fan the flame of interest in this unique direction? The present education is moulded around sustaining, expanding and supporting the present social standing, a complex status quo, fashioned and nurtured over many years. Its extensive roots reach back over long periods of applied thinking, experience, intentions and social experiment. In this there have been many years of spiritual denial under the dominion of the mind, ever busy, at the helm of human affairs. Not love of our spiritual nature accorded the higher value but love of the state, of the nation and its traditions and a deep obsession with individual expansion and achievement within the social framework.

So we have the mind at work, at play, organising, arranging — the eager vanguard of an energetic assault on life, on nature, brushing aside sensitive considerations about the deeper meaning of existence while it pursues its social and individual establishment. Security-ridden minds, steeped in separation, seeking to mould the delicate artistry of life into supportive patterns of protection that deny the essential unity of mankind. Isolation and division on the rampage in time, fragmenting the human race, building barriers of language, race, colour, religion, social and political ideas — gathering humans together in disjointed sections and vying one against the other for enrichment, power, control and a more secure place under the social sun.

Education is slanted to foster division and separation, to exalt the individual aspect of the human expression through achievement, through emphasis and distinction. Education that supports spiritual discovery is denied the encouragement it needs to turn the human race away from the present entanglements in time and head towards the Great Unknown, towards a new purpose in living, to a new and different foundation to build on. With the demands of the mind running riot, unchecked by a natural spiritual discipline, so the forces of darkness, of violence, destruction and disarrangement find ready outlets. And neither fear of the consequences, nor retribution, nor public outcry have been able to eradicate the flow of violent expression.

It will take a new kind of education to do this. The response of armed might can blunt its momentum but this also feeds the intensity of the conflagration and leaves humans always in a state of preparedness, wondering when the next outbreak will be. Mankind either continues in this manner or, realising the tragic consequences of doing so, develops a new approach. One that builds on the basis of our universal spiritual nature rather than the projected inventions and arrangements of mind intent on preserving the present social directions and its adopted standing in the social mainstream.

In the mind, there is not unity, little of peace and gentleness and much of prejudice, self-centred considerations and self seeking. The disruption we observe comes from the mind and its accumulated background. In mind devoid of spiritual discovery lie the seeds of violence through the way it thinks, operates and reacts. The seeds are nurtured deep in the mind. Fertilised with ill will and misunderstanding, they grow into a harvest of reactionary endeavour. Where they are given birth, it is there they will have to wither and die, before the growth takes off and expands into explosive action. By then it is too late and the damage is done.

Education, to help out, must take those who are interested as deeply as possible into the inner workings of the mind. Here, in the shadowy reaches that are the breeding ground for the twisted, unbalanced thinking that guides violence on its painful way, is where the means have to be brought to bear to banish it from the human expression. Talk, education, reading are only the first steps. Explanations cannot take us into the complex and intricate world of the mind. It needs a deep and sustained interest to unravel the incredible reactions and judgements going on and a shift in the focus of attention from the outer to the inner. And many a helping hand from that high level which is the universal witness of all that we think and do.

While mankind continues in the customary directions and travels the usual byways of timeful experience with energetic endeavour, that is all that will open out and the inner contents of the human expression will remain a closed book, never opened, never read. Eager interest, heartfelt intention have the capacity to turn the attention away from its outer focus and inwards to explore unseen reaches of the human psyche. This may take a little time to settle for it is not easy to change long years of ingrained habit. With happy persistence, a rapport opens up with the inner and this side of the human expression begins to reveal its contents, the influences and the motives that shape its behaviour and outlook on life.

This is new territory to travel in, one of establishment and expansion, of underlying power control, of a constant input being absorbed and incorporated, added to the mind's collection for use, protection and as a reference library to exploit when necessary. It is here the spiritual student must venture to understand the self's behaviour. We cannot be conscious travellers in these depths in the usual way we experience happenings on the surface where the continuous flow of events has its particular and well-known imprint. But it sometimes happens that the barriers of relativity fall away, the spiritual steps in to lend a hand and the mind loses its familiar standing. That's when deep insights into hidden aspects of the mind's nature leap with revelatory impact into the mind's field of awareness.

To briefly experience this temporary loss of the individual standing is to shift suddenly from intellectual confrontation with life. What has been entrenched in the body expands from the restrictions of a sense-based standpoint, disentangles itself from the effects of experience, from its accumulation of attitudes and knowledge and the limiting effects of words and thinking. The vast background base, good, bad or neutral is put aside. The human expression is spring cleaned of every aspect it formerly seemed to be. It is in a brand new state without imprint of any kind, mental, emotional or physical. The spiritual sparkle of life has responded to the seeker's earnest endeavours and absorbed the individual nature deep into its own. In that moment, little self is purged of its littleness and its isolation.

Barriers of ignorance and misunderstanding are shattered by this reunion. The contents of the mind are exposed in sharp relief. Out into the open they come, translated directly into a means clear to the surface mind. This is the beginning of a new learning, a new education — one that gains its impetus from beyond the mind. The seeds are set in spiritual discovery, in that unified state of being where the mind is not as an observer relative to some experience. It is a dynamic uprisal affecting every level of the human expression, from its deepest foundations and extending upwards and outwards where it is so well established in its individual standing, in polarities and relativity and where relationships hold powerful sway.

No other learning can affect human nature so profoundly nor open it up to introspection so effectively and clearly. Violent intentions, dark, brooding moods, self-centred urges melt away like a block of ice in a roaring inferno. And whatever Self does from then on, whatever patterns of behaviour are set up in response to this spiritual discovery and to the challenges of life, these too are relentlessly exposed by the light of this higher standing. There is no stopping the process that takes off once it is on its way.

Self can never return to the former arrangements that prevailed unchallenged. Nor can it return to the former limited standing now banished forever to the pages of past endeavour. It is now alive like never before, eager to go on with its learning. An imperious directive is abroad, urging constant investigation of every impulse and pattern that settles in to lay any sort of claim to the self. Anything based on personal profit or return for its own sake, these too are soon dealt with. Everything is grist to the spiritual mills as they turn and nurture a growing back into the universal. Here is the true meaning of evolution — the culmination of the spiritual till it sweeps all before it and remakes individuals into shining examples of its own sparkling nature.

6.

LIVING as an individual is deeply ingrained and difficult to put aside. It has fashioned its imprint deep in the human expression. Humans no longer look simply, in full awareness at the nature they are but look instead at the covering garments that conceal their true nature. Accordingly, they act to protect the structures, believing that in so doing they are truly protecting the most vital aspect of what they are. Imbued in the psyche are the attitudes that the life and the appearance we know as the self are of the highest importance and value. We hold to these, not only outwardly where the dangers to self-survival are appreciated but also inwardly where the psychological hold to mental constructs is tenaciously deep rooted. Mind does not easily give over its positions of prominence in these directions.

We will always nurture the structures that give substance and meaning to the mind. They are the gateways into timeful living, the means by which humans express their intentions in the world of experience. But there is nothing going on to balance the over emphasis on the individual side and its ever expanding ramifications. This absorbs all the attention, leaving little for spiritual exploration. With this over emphasis on the outer and support of the outer by the inner, the spiritual side is ignored and access denied to its purifying stream of universal awareness. The capacity to spark off renewal and regeneration doesn't get a chance. The movement of an unrestricted understanding is dammed back by the relentless intellectual movement of a mind expressing its intentions through the background of knowledge and experience gained from an isolated standpoint which lacks any input from the universal side of existence.

Living revolves far too much around the determinations, demands and desires of the mind. Everything coming through the mind must be sanctioned and supported by the mind. This includes a range of intentions, feelings and actions. Whatever festers deep within comes out eventually, including violent outpourings of diverse natures. Could society stem this flow by verbal education or even by exemplary behaviour? Could laws, no matter how thoughtfully constructed, dam it back at its source before it explodes with negative energy on the human scene? How could outsiders, from a distant standpoint, be aware of the precise moment when deranged behaviour is about to be transformed from idea or impulse to direct and destructive action?

The ideas, impulses and intentions that form are best surveyed and understood by the minds concerned. Directly, not second hand through a verbal mirror or descriptive screen offered by another. No matter how well intentioned those who understand their part in the human drama nor how explicitly they explain the deeper workings of the mind, they cannot lead another into the deeper stages of self-discovery. They encourage, support and inspire a sustained interest but those stirred to venture this way must cast off all the attachments that bind them to factual knowledge, to verbal descriptions and reasonable explanations and travel inwards without teacher or experience, guidelines or pathways. The inner territory has no stepping stones, no familiar landmarks. Nor does it normally give conscious indication of the nature of what is going on until we are uplifted to an elevated spiritual standing. Then we see by an expanded light the nature of what is involved.

Humans must go inwards to get to the root of their troubles, to solve problems caused by a lack of love and understanding. Out of conscious sight does not mean non-existent or non-acting. Humans are quick to recognise the self-evident, the obvious impact, and understandably so. What registers on the mind is all that it is concerned with. The effort to delve into the mystery of life and mind is an attempt to bring into the conscious register what was formerly inferred or marginally suspected. Though we deepen knowledge of the self to a certain extent through reason, the truth of what goes on in the mind's depth is gained by a different approach. Otherwise it loses much of its uniqueness through reasonable interpretation based on a distant standpoint rather than from moments of integration when inner and outer come together, unity reigns and revelation makes clear what reason failed to see.

Reasonable images are acceptable to a degree, more so when they are projections of the realities they represent, but they cannot be accepted as bona fide presentations of what actually takes place. They are imitations, not the originals. Like the image in a photograph they are only a copy. The original happening is integrated at the creative moment of arisal. This is the take-off state of human behaviour in the unconscious. The projection on the surface appears separate, is acknowledged and appraised as a conscious happening, connected and relative to the observer as a separate experience.

This is why we do not usually observe the beginning of a violent reaction stirring, nor of any action while it is germinating in the unconscious. Only the conscious result gives evidence of the quality of the expression set in motion. By then, humans are locked into a relative situation and are either under its control, or move to act to subdue its effects or intended effects through resistance or imposed discipline.

The manner in which the mind works in time is the biggest barrier to spiritual learning. Influenced by habit, tradition, experience and its accumulation of material to operate along restricted lines of thinking and project actions that agree with its determinations, Mind finds it difficult to shift out of the accustomed grooves it travels in. Nothing new is allowed to intrude unless it meets with the mind's approval. While the mind stands as sentinel in charge of the daily movement of material in and out of the precinct of the self, so the decisions made will conform to the dominant influences or fears that exist within the mind.

7.

TO pursue this line of inquiry inevitably brings the mind into contact with social and individual conditioning. It is through these two waves of imposed influences that controlling screens are set up to monitor incoming information, digest it, and determine present or future courses of action. This appraisal may be conscious and slower or carried out subconsciously with almost lightning-like speed. Reactions follow from decisions made from here. With the intention to contain violence, the background content from which it arises to spill out into surface living must be thoroughly understood. Analysis of the outer causes of violence gives only a marginal understanding of the situation arising. This leads to conditions of control that are at best limited in degree and scope. The problem keeps recurring and never fades away.

The best solution lies in a different direction. This begins with reasonable analysis, reflection, discussion and observation, but does not become effective until it shifts into the realm of spiritual discovery. Reasonable introspection is a powerful factor in the human approach to understanding its problems. But this cannot lay bare the underlying nature of the human expression with the crystal clarity and insights released by reconnecting with the spiritual. When this is fully active, self prejudice or misinterpretation of the facts is not permitted to intrude and distort the obvious. The meaning of the situation in question simply comes through, just as it is.

Those in whom a spiritual awakening is active are in the best position of naturally controlling their own behaviour. The understanding that takes off, the love that is awakened, deals with the challenges that come their way with a minimum of fuss. Likewise, those who make it their business or profession to deal with those who transgress would be even better equipped than they now are if spiritual awareness was allied to their considerable experience and expertise in these matters.

Where spiritual discovery is absent or limited in its function, so understanding revolves around a lesser level of comprehension and tends to serve the interests and intentions of the lesser self. In those easily swayed towards disruption, this means prejudice, ambition, rampant desires and sudden impulses or base consideration in a mind which convinces itself to do what the seductive whispers of reason suggest for whatever purposes.

The power of the self to persist in any medium is a factor not always taken into account by those who seek to regulate human behaviour. When the self is harnessed to support the prevailing social conditions and does not in any way act as a disruptive influence, its energetic endeavours are welcomed and not interrogated. It is when it falls out of line, reflecting unwanted social behaviour, that the tools of reason are brought to bear on the consequences that arise when humans transgress the accepted social standards. The disruptive impact that follows is disturbing enough to draw reflection and action from those whose business it is to act on such matters. They draw from a pool of experience and expertise in dealing with the situations and people involved. This has developed over long years of social interaction.

As new ways of treatment are developed they are incorporated into the background pool. But in spite of considerable changes over the years in how humans think and deal with violence and irrational behaviour, in the dealing out of justice, the tendency towards violence in one form or another is not rapidly moving downwards. It is still with us, not only in the incidents that arise, in the brutality reflected against defenceless people, the constant use of highly destructive weapons on the fields of war, but also in the political arenas where savage verbal violence reverberates across the floor. All this makes the sensitive wonder just when mankind is going to wake from its self-created stupor, realign the self with the spiritual and bring to an end all the ugly ways that have predominated with the denial of love, of integration, of the unity they share with the Spiritual Strangeness.

Without this and the light it sheds on human living we are lost sheep without direction, and know not what to do for relief nor where to go. We drift from one difficulty to another but our dark side pursues us wherever we go. And so it will, till we turn, face what we have allowed ourselves to become, acknowledge this and reach out for the light that waits beyond the mind. This is the only salvation.

CONCLUSION

DURING its long journey along the highways and byways of timeful living, the human expression has been accompanied by a shadowy twin self — our unruly friend, alter ego. The lost and lonely one, looking for somewhere to lay down its troubled burden and come to rest in peaceful and happy living. Dark indeed have been the stains left by alter ego. Pain-filled its journey. All kinds of disarranged living, debaucheries, tortures and cruelties inflicted beyond belief. Killing and destruction. Such an unhappy creature is alter ego.

Riddled with fear, apprehensive of danger lurking behind every shadow, uncertain of its place in the universal movement, desperate at all costs to hold onto something, anything that yields a feeling or vision of substance. Terrified of being reduced to a nonentity, our shadowy self suffers from a most grievous illness — lack of love. This has been the basis of all the disarranged behaviour reflected over the years. Whatever it is, whatever has been done in the service of shadowy alter ego has been done because it is not enfolded in the warm security of love, has not experienced what love is all about. So it wanders this earthly home cut off from the richest, most nourishing source of all — that of the love the universal holds for its human children.

Denied access by its own actions, by its wilful insistence to go it alone, relying on its own limited resources, it degenerated into a shrunken creature, a caricature of the wonderful expression it was meant to be. The angelic side within is covered by a shadowy overtone bent on self-torture, even on the destruction of its own kind. It brings a devilish ingenuity to bear to serve this bent for destruction through its willing servant, intellectual reason. Organised and harnessed by sinister and misguided intent, the mind's creative genius has devised machines of unparalleled destruction and used them to enslave or destroy fellow humans.

That is the behaviour displayed by intellectual mind in the service of the shadowy twin — the one who would usurp its role in the human expression and become the master of all it surveys rather than the servant of love, the compliant instrument of a spiritual intention to reawaken mankind to its original angelic nature. Sad indeed have been the results of this schism in the human expression. Sundered from its spiritual source by its blind intransigence, its infatuation with appearance and the illusion of separation, shadowy twin has gone on an unbridled rampage of unseemly behaviour.

So many have been hurt, have needlessly suffered in its service. Love was never far away. Closer indeed than a touch or a breath, waiting to reclaim its errant child. Forgiveness too was waiting for it, if only it would turn from its mind-driven rush towards serving the shadowy side, its quirky appetites and devious ways and return to the universal fold.

For those who break free from the shadowy self's tenacious hold, the welcome mat is always out where love rules by divine expression. And it is love, universal love and this alone that eases shadowy self out of the way, dispelling its dark overtones and flooding it with the light that ends its disruptive ways, making in its place a reflection of the light — a light Being. Filled with this, alive with this, brimful of the Sunshine of Love, the new-found self says goodbye to shadowy self. The dark has been loved out of existence and new self is abroad. Goodbye violence, goodbye strange and erratic behaviour. Welcome gentleness, affection, fun-filled days and togetherness in being.

Is this just a dream? Try it and see. Turn away from shadowy self. Put aside everything it is, that issues from it. Stand silently at that mystic, inner door that is the entrance to love. Stand naked, without embellishments, protection or desire, without any movement that comes from shadowy self. With the shadowy one out of the way, the Sunshine of Love comes shining through to warm up the human heart like nothing else can. The tears will flow. Let them. Don't hold back. A cleansing power will sweep through. The agony of all the past, long years of separation, the stunted, limited living, the memories of pain and suffering, of so many wrongs done, for and against — all will be washed away.

Joy and delight will walk this earth. Smiles will break out. Love will reach out its hands to love. Love will embrace love. What formerly paraded as shadowy self will cast aside its dark reflection and revel in its incredible good fortune. It will now belong to the Sunshine of Love, is indeed of the very same nature. No more need for all the past actions. The new will be abroad.

So be it for all those who reach out for the Sunshine of Love. For assuredly it will come their way, sometime, somehow.

About the author

JOSEPH RAFFA WAS born in 1927 in Fremantle, Western Australia. He enjoyed an idyllic childhood roaming the bush and the seashore. In his teens Joseph became a dedicated atheist, looking to science for answers to the riddles of life and the universe. Then, in his early twenties, he experienced a moment of discovery that transformed his life. As Joseph's life opened out spiritually following this awakening, he was inspired to put pen to paper to encourage others to embark on their own journey of discovery.

Joseph died of cancer in 2010, leaving behind a legacy of inspirational writing which is now being made available to a wider audience. Visit www.towardsthesilentheart.com for more information about Joseph and his books.

Other books by Joseph Raffa

Beside Still Waters

ISBN 9780987227676

This beautiful collection of essays touches on the universal search for meaning and inspires readers to reach out for the still waters of the spirit.

The human heart longs for peace and harmony. It seeks a restful haven from the relentless busyness of everyday life, drawing us to spend tranquil moments in natural surrounds that offer a brief respite from the hustle and bustle. There is a state of inner stillness, when the endless chatter of the mind has ceased, that a deeper understanding arises. These are the 'still waters' that bring new life to mankind, that lay claim to the heart and redirect the mind. These are the waters of peace, love and true togetherness that lift us up to divine heights of being and living.

The Silent Guardian

ISBN 9780987227669

A timely reminder of our spiritual journey and true purpose on Earth.

Joseph shares an inspirational message for those who care to listen.

Explore the planets, the outer reaches of space, the depths of the seas. Burrow into the earth, climb every mountain. When you have seen it all, you will still be left with the mystery of yourself. Turn and face this. Explore this. When you've travelled the extent and depth of the human expression, much of what you learn will be beyond the mind's capacity to convey through verbalisation. When heart speaks to heart, what more is there to say?

The Silent Guardian

Beyond the Cross

The Christ Collection

ISBN 9780987227652

A moving collection of inspired pieces about Jesus.

Joseph Raffa was a dedicated atheist when he set out in search of answers to the riddles of life and the universe. Then, in a blissful moment of discovery, the God the Bible speaks of, the Allah of Mohammed and the longed for Nirvana of the Buddhists came into his life. As his life opened out spiritually, Joseph began to have a deeper appreciation of Jesus, His life and His role in the spiritual awakening of Mankind. Visions and insights arose unbidden, in such a manner that their authenticity could not be questioned. The young man who was an atheist for a time, who cared not to read the Bible or take much notice of Christ and His life, found himself anchored in God and also writing pieces extolling the virtues, the wisdom and the love expressed by that super spiritual being of long ago.

Thank you for taking the time to read this book. Ratings and reviews are appreciated. If you enjoyed it, please Tweet/Share on your social media networks.

www.ingramcontent.com/pod-product-compliance
Lightning Source LLC
Chambersburg PA
CBHW060723030426
42337CB00017B/2984